LeRoy Neiman '94

LeROY NEIMAN

ON SAFARI

To Dave

LeRoy Neiman

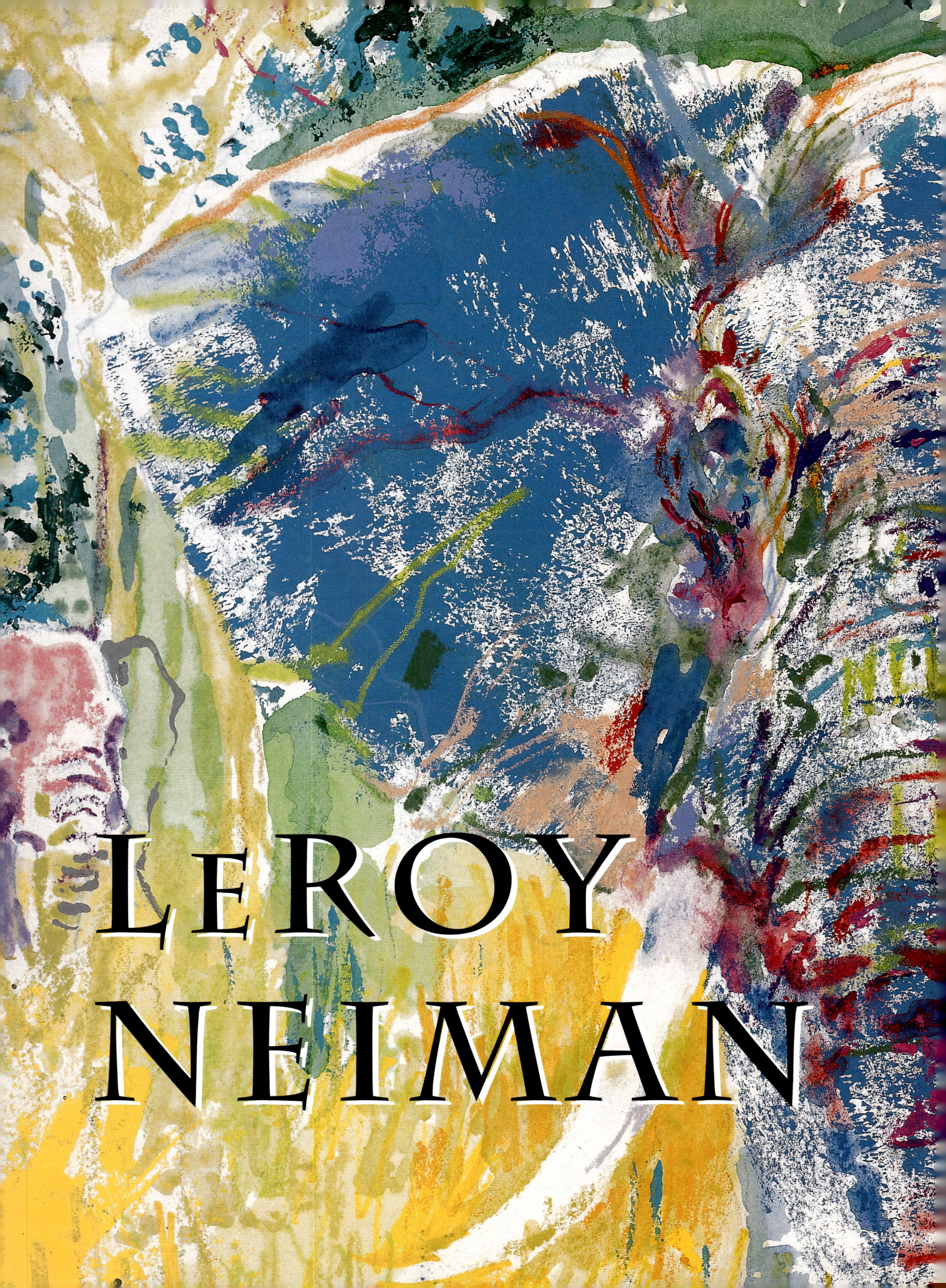
LeROY
NEIMAN

ON
SAFARI
HARRY N. ABRAMS, INC., PUBLISHERS

Editor: Adele Westbrook
Designer: Liz Trovato

Library of Congress Cataloging-in-Publication Data
Neiman, LeRoy, 1927–
LeRoy Neiman on safari.
p. cm.
ISBN 0–8109–6332–9 (clothbound)
1. Mammals—Kenya. 2. Big game animals—Kenya. 3. Safaris—Kenya. 4. Mammals—Kenya—Pictorial works. 5. Big game animals—Kenya—Pictorial works. 6. Safaris—Kenya—Pictorial works.
I. Title.
QL731.K46N44 1997
599.096762—dc20 96–25980

Published in 1997 by Harry N. Abrams, Incorporated, New York
A Times Mirror Company

Printed and bound in Italy

Contents

THE BIG FIVE

PROLOGUE

This is about the lion, elephant, cape buffalo, rhinoceros, and leopard. The Big Five—two carnivores, three grazers.

These celebrity subjects of the great African game preserves in their natural environment, inhabit a stupendous landscape steeped in fantasy and danger. A vast stage made up of endless sweeping golden plains, green escarpments, scattered trees, scarce watering holes, winding rivers, and swamps, it is habitat to a domain of wild animals coexisting, reproducing, and striving to survive. Their weapons are teeth, claws, hooves, horns, and tusks—prey and predators alike.

I set off for equatorial Africa not as a hunter looking to bag trophies, nor as a photographer shooting game. Any shooting was left to our accompanying video crew.

I made on-location studies while being bounced and thrown about, standing in a mezzanine-like lookout position rolling along, sighting game atop a powerful, intimidating (Humvee) Hummer, the Rolls-Royce of the bush, a heavy tank-like vehicle that was created in response to the needs of the Gulf War. I lay no claim to being an adventurer, a Hemingway, a Teddy Roosevelt, a William Holden or such. I came here to draw and paint what I see, and express how I feel.

This book is a selection of work compiled on a three-week bloodless safari and gives evidence of how an artist observes animals as a dedicated amateur, while experiencing the dream-like, seemingly endless beauty of life on the savannah—and its constant peril.

In preparation, before departing from New York for the Kenya animal kingdom, I visited the American Museum of Natural History dioramas in the African Animal Hall, viewing the lifelike taxidermy examples of the Big Five.

As a wrap-up, upon the conclusion of our safari, I checked out the Natural History Museum in Nairobi, where stuffed animals stand in the open to be studied in the round, thinking all the while about the wild animals imprisoned in zoos and habitats, deprived of the stalking of the hunt, of gathering their own food, of the freedom to roam about, and mate with selection, as these preserved specimens once did.

The portable field materials I chose for the portrayal of the Big Five were charcoal for chiaroscuro rendering on standard drawing sheets, pen and ink for quick jottings, plus felt-tip markers and watercolor for my personal sketchbook. The challenge was eased by mild, soft breezes and the fragrant August air, under high, forever clear blue skies. Our pursuits fit perfectly between fiery sunrises and sunsets, which is prime time in animal land.

A pair of six- by twelve-feet primed canvases, some sixty acrylic and enamel cans of colors, watercolor tubes and pans, plus painting gear had preceded me from New York. A film crew had also been imported from Los Angeles to record the adventure. There will be no beating around the bush out here. The bush is my outdoor studio. It's now time to get it on.

Upon landing in Nairobi at the Jomo Kenyatta International Airport, we had immediately boarded a small Cesna 407—final destination a private grass-covered airstrip near Nanyuki.

The command post where we marshaled our forces was Robert Halmi, Sr.'s compound, the Mt. Kenya Safari Ranch. Its animal orphanage is adjacent to the opulent Mt. Kenya Safari Club that offers tennis court nets smack on the equator. Early mornings, it provided a thrilling panoramic view of Mt. Kenya, Africa's second-highest peak, proudly making its majestic appearance. For what seemed no more than an hour, the mountain would show its royal headdress, then shyly hide behind the clouds for the remainder of the day.

The first day out in a swamp, sketching elephants scattered out as far as the eye could see, we discovered straightaway that it is possible to drive in amongst a herd of swaying elephant or the unpredictable cape buffalo. They can be aloof, scatter, or charge—no guarantee. I wore a baseball-like cap and recalled photos of Hemingway on safari showing him favoring such a cap but with a deeper, longer-billed visor. Thinking about Hemingway as we rolled through bog and slough axle deep, a terrain that seems to suit the elephant, I remembered reading his first African book, *The Green Hills of Africa*, and how yellow the contour of the distant savannah and hills seemed. True, the escarpments were greenish, but it was basically a Dakota grain field gold to me. Then again, maybe it was just that time of year.

The animals live in open freedom. There are no "no trespassing" signs. I feel like an intruder invading their privacy as if they are fair game. We approach a resting, yawning lion luxuriating on his belly in tall grass. I succeed in catching his gaze as I work away at a charcoal, doing what's called a "contour drawing." At art school classes that means not looking at your paper while drawing. I lock eyes, eyeball to eyeball with the noble beast, my heart pounding. He stares me down unblinking with cool detached indifference for a long spell, then breaking his pose, he flops over on his side and falls asleep.

Drawing an animal must be an honest undertaking. In the sanctuary of the wilds both carnivores and grazers face truth and reality every minute. If they are hungry or thirsty, they just are. If they, the carnivores, have a full stomach, that too is reality and renders them satisfied, lazy, and not dangerous, which relaxes nearby grazers.

Drawing thorny acacia trees, escarpments, and unique landscape details is one thing, but you can't draw wild animals with any confidence or understanding without doing reams of drawings of them live.

To arrive at a certain mastery of the human figure, art schools have figure drawing classes so that students can arrive at a better understanding of the human body and its gestures. If the artist wants to get the hang of drawing animals in natural surroundings, then drawing them live in their environment is a necessity—it makes all the difference. Sketching at zoos or strictly from photographs just doesn't cut it.

The artist benefits in awe from the experience of seeing wildlife in natural surroundings . . . notices what they notice as they ignore or react to different situations and stimuli . . . observes their moves when they scheme, conspire, maneuver . . . notes not so much their reaction to the expected but to the unexpected. You come to love these creatures of God. Their freedom is contagious. It gets to you early and maintains its hold.

LeRoy Neiman '94

The Big Five

PORTRAITS

Lion

Elephant

Cape Buffalo

Rhinoceros

Leopard

Lion

The lion is plentiful and leads a life free of threat. The King of Beasts in animal land is royalty purring or growling.

Elephant

The elephant is the heavyweight champion with no challengers, the world's largest land mammal. When disturbed while browsing or on the move, elephants will charge, trumpeting.

Cape Buffalo

The cape buffalo, against a backdrop of Mt. Kenya, is a vicious, vindictive, threatening, brooding, and potent ruminant. Called "iron-like" by Isak Dinesen in the very beginning pages of her book *Out of Africa*.

Rhinoceros

The white rhinoceros has two horns on its snout. The front nasal protuberance can be as long as four feet. In contrast, it has a pair of rather delicate tulip-shaped ears. In Ionesco's play *Rhinoceros*, the rhino running full-tilt was described as "unicorned."

Leopard

The leopard, strictly upper class, is the most elegant of the larger felines—a graceful and slick nocturnal stalker with a distinctive, handsome round head. Being a loner, it is always showtime when this *danseur étoile* appears.

LeRoy Neiman
'95

(Opposite page, above)
I'm sketching the rhino in profile when the second one comes circling around from behind the canvas.

(Opposite page, below)
Then they horn in on my painting to check out their likenesses.

(This page, above)
Doing a lion drawing.

(This page, below)
Elephant walk.

The Lion

Fabled, ferocious, savage yet dignified.
Hemingway once said, "The big cats are the eternal stars."
The lion's share seems to be his right. This is lion land.

LeRoy Neiman '94

A tawny golden yellowish in keeping with the landscape.
Thus blended they have the advantage

Lion live 8 to 10 years in the wild + 25 years in captivity

Monarch
Male 500 lbs

In the open large animals don't bother looking upward.
They have nothing to fear from above
STAKE-OUT

Male, Lioness
and Cubs

Lion legend—in Medieval art, the lion was a symbol of the Resurrection of Christ. It was believed that when the lion gave birth, its offspring were born dead and were brought to life by a parent breathing on them. Venetians of the Serenissima chose this mightiest of beasts as their symbol. British heraldry adopted the lion for their official coat of arms.

Lion family

The Elephant

Talk about the heart of the lion—how about the big-hearted elephant. The pachyderm's heart weighs sixty pounds.

1st Day
Swamp

Browsers

These mighty, peace-loving gentle giants lumber on the soles of soft, spongy feet.

Pink Elephant

RIO DE ORO
FRENCH

the shape of the Elephant's ear is that of the continent of Africa.
ANGLO-EGYPTIAN
SUDAN
ETHIOPIA
KENYA
BELGIAN
CONGO
ANGOLA
SOUTH AFRICA

Side by side
side to side

Brick red coloration from soil

Kilimanjaro Bulls

Mount Kilimanjaro, Africa's hightest peak, towers behind two posturing bulls.

The Cape Buffalo

Ill-tempered, vicious, ponderous, slow-trekking grazers.

Solid, dull.
Candidate for distinction as the most dangerous animal on the continent, plus a five-foot horn spread, made this bovine a popular trophy for big game hunters.

Largest of the cattlelike hoofed mammals
Herds dominated by a bull but led by a Cow

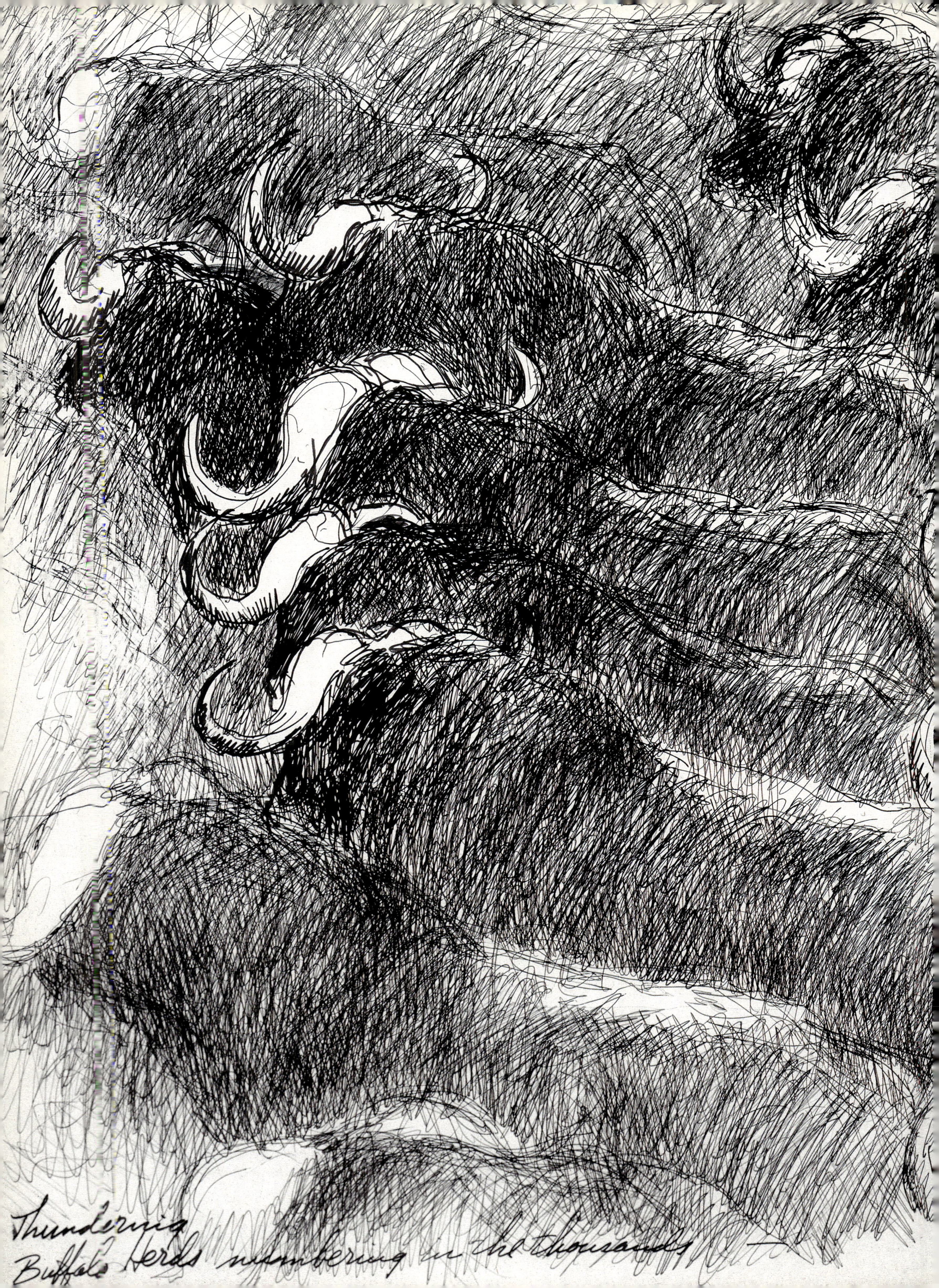
Thundering
Buffalo Herds numbering in the thousands

3rd Day
LeRoy Neiman
Kenya '94

THE RHINOCEROS

Endangered remnant of an ancient world. Contemporary of the dinosaur. Heavy-headed. Can be seven feet at shoulder. Poor eyesight, acute sense of hearing and smell. Creature of routine.

Rhino life expectancy is 40 years.
while the elephant never forgets, the Rhino has a short memory

The Leopard

Ancients proclaimed leopards to be animals of the moon, while lions were animals of the sun. The rare lion and leopard offspring are called leopon.

The elusive, imperial leopard, solitary, blends into the tree's leaves and shadows.

The spotted cat out on a limb, but camouflaged. Calculating, patient, persistent.

Head round - spots on head enlarge - then turn to rosettes

Luxurious long whiskers
on body

It is always wise
when near or under trees to
check overhead.

LeRoy Neiman '75

ZEBRA

GIRAFFE

BABOON

ANIMAL LAND

MONKEY

WARTHOG

CHEETAH

WILDEBEEST

HIPPOPOTAMUS

THE ZEBRA

The noisy zebra loves to run, gallop, and canter, finding safety in close gatherings.

Unlikely?
Herbivore at water with carnivore?
Do the antelope and zebra trust
that the lapping lioness has recently dined
and is only thirsty?
Maybe the artist, too long under a
baking sun, could use a long cool drink.

Zebra variation of striping — runs 40 mph

Zebra family

The Giraffe

The aristocratic, stately giraffe, eighteen to twenty feet in height, is the thoroughbred of the plains. Giraffes can run tirelessly up to thirty mph. Their front hooves are deadly defense weapons. Big game hunters and poachers found them too tall for trophies, their meat not tasty, and their hides not in demand.

(Above, left)
The male performs his topiary art by pruning the thorny acacia trees as high as his neck can stretch, leveling the branches flat across the bottom.

(Above and below, right)
The female does her gardening by bending over and nibbling grass stems.

(Opposite page)
A decorative flagstone-patterned giraffe family.

The Baboon

Baboons have a poodle-like head with razor-sharp teeth. Always curious, they pick up edibles and eat them daintily with their hands. Not to be overlooked—these characters being so closely related to us.

most agile powerful tail

fighter – French Poodle Look

highly intelligent Politely take their food to their mouths with their hands when eating

Baboon

... the monkey is protected by ...

Troop of foraging baboons.

The Monkey

Primates are seemingly everywhere. A community of vervet monkeys chatter, screech, climb, swing, cling, leap, and chase one another. Tempers flare, then the next minute they are grooming each other. The frisky monkeys seem to be always bickering or finding one another sexually attractive. The monkey makes the most of a fifteen-year life span. They have elaborate brains, acute binocular vision, and forward-facing eyes for depth perception.

Excellent thieves

THE WARTHOG

Another smaller animal entered in my sketchbook, the irresistible warthog. Sturdy, sprightly, and Napoleonic, it briskly trots, struts, and scurries. This chesty pugnacious pig is powerful and combative.

Structured like a miniature rhino, the feisty, appealing omnivore has been observed wallowing in mud baths together with his huge counterpart.

warthog - suspicious / what he does not
understand he suspects

The Cheetah

An eye-catching standout is the sleek cheetah. Their life expectancy is four to five years—no wonder the tear rivulets seem to run down the sides of their small, kittenish faces. Lithe, dazzling, graceful, the cheetah has been clocked at seventy mph. A sprinter, he overheats and tires easily, symbolically running out of time into extinction.

Most dog-like of cats, and a daytime hunter—the cheetah's claws are not retractable.

Maasai Mara Kenya
04

As with domestic cats, the Cheetah can pay
little or no attention to man's presence.

LeRoy Neiman '95

THE WILDEBEEST

Wildebeest scamper about like adolescents, just for the joy of moving, kick up their heels, gallop in a sort of rocking horse stiffness, and fake being furiously angry. There is nothing endangered about these kicky multitudes, who number in the many thousands.

Acrobatic

A romping, zanny cut-up
the gnu is a buffalo-faced
horse-tailed antelope.
Appears a hold-over from
a pre-historic geological past.

The Hippopotamus

At camp, I sketched the ever-present hippopotamus. The drawings were done outside my tent overlooking a roly-poly pileup—laid out, constantly changing position, submerging themselves in the muddy brown Mara River only to resurface and plop down again in an ever-rearranging configuration of listless but restless blubber.

However good-natured a river pileup may appear, if a quarrel between two rival male hippos should occur it can result in a fight to the death, the winner shredding the remains of his opponent.

Tourists and guides usually have the bush scene much to themselves. Camping and field trips hold little fascination for the native Kenyans. The youth of Kenya and their modern, comfort-oriented elders generally do not frequent these wildlife locales, perceiving little recreational value in safari expeditions. Besides finding that safaris are unaffordable, perhaps they sense that the wild animals are free while they are not! It may be that the wide-open spaces offer a counterpoint to their own lives, cooped up in their modern urban dwellings. Maybe they realize that they have relatively little freedom to make decisions and choices of their own, as compared to their untamable neighbors in the wild.

The artist as safarist gets a little wacky along the way, as he meddles around this environment relating and reflecting while sketching. In the romantic raw, while studying the social attitudes and behavior patterns of these tenants of the bush, an anthropomorphic tempta-

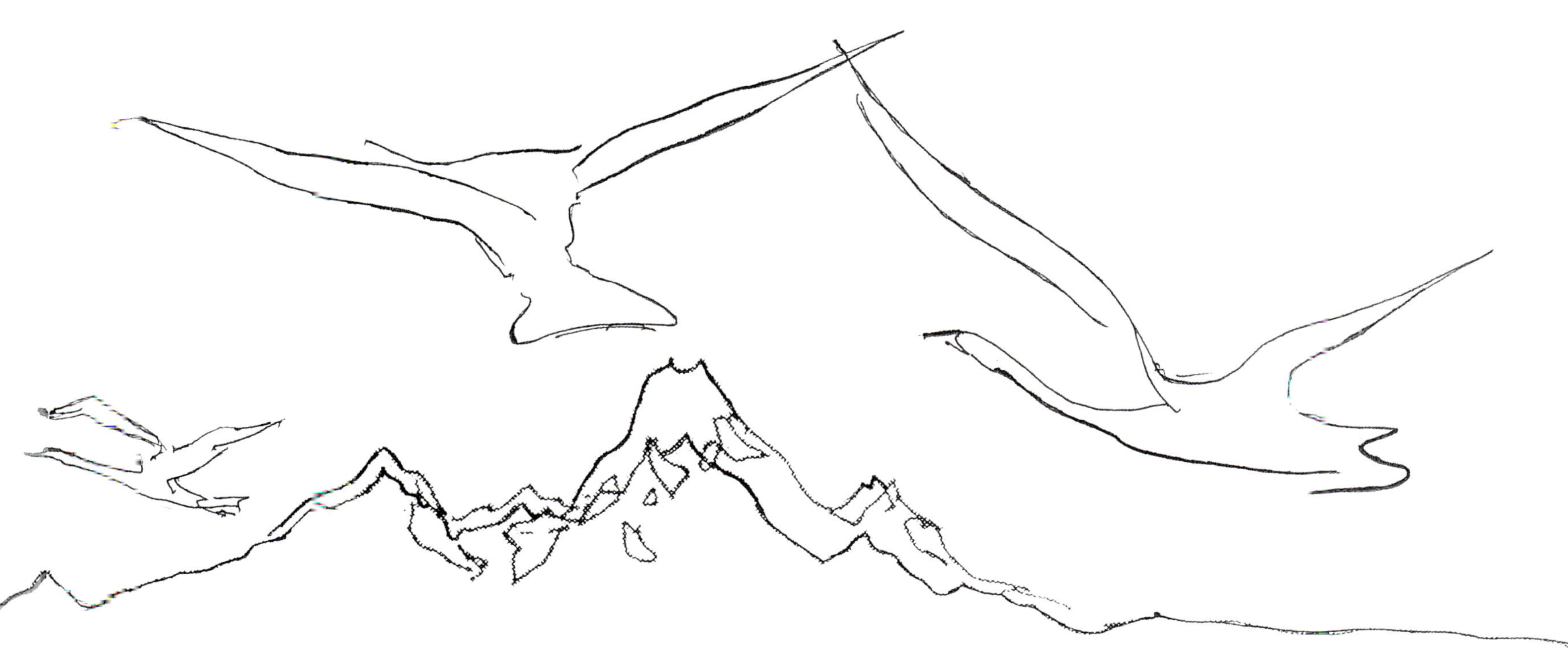

tion tends to arise. The question renews itself. Do you attribute to these magnificent prolific creatures under scrutiny, emotions, goals, consciousness, intelligence, or other characteristics viewed as exclusively human, based on their inherent dignity? Being so close, but unable to touch, there is the desire to explore their inner world—forget it.

With man and beast sharing the same environment, acquiring their own food and defenses collectively or individually, one comes to the conclusion that the bush is no place to draw facile comparisons. It is strictly an opportunity to appreciate the nature and intelligence of the animals.

Who gets the nod? The animal who never accomplished human achievements? Or is man's greatest accomplishment his refusal to do what the beast within him wills?

. . . Maybe I'd better stick to my drawing . . .

THE CAMP

camp Kitchen Mara River private Camp Kenya/East Africa
on the Hippo cliffs

Along the picturesque Mara River, we are occupying the same campsite where the *African Queen* was filmed in 1951.

Every evening as we are having after-dinner *digestifs* around the campfire under the stars, dozens of baboons fill the branches of the same large acacia tree across the river from us. As the hippos move onto land to do their nocturnal grazing, stark white egrets descend to roost along the banks. They take flight at the first sign of daybreak, as we are taking breakfast in the large dining tent.

While we slept, the action out there had not subsided. Like New York, the city that never sleeps, the carnivores prowl and hunt by moonlight throughout the night.

(Jock Anderson Camp)

Our camp was lavish compared to my recall of army bivouac areas: Private tents with showers (hand-filled with hot water), latrines, and electric light bulbs. We enjoyed international and regional cuisine suited to the palate of the most sophisticated traveler . . . fit for a maharaja on tiger shikar or a royal partridge shoot in the Scottish Highlands . . . with wine and champagne selections, foie gras, fresh-baked bread, crème brûlée, and the like.

Compared to my hitch as an army cook in World War II, the field kitchen with its twenty-four-hour round-the-clock, all-purpose stove was a wonder in its own right. It was made up of white-hot coals gracefully structured on ten years' worth of ashes, about three feet high by three feet wide and probably eight feet long . . . its flat top served as a grill, and as a baking and roasting oven with a ten-gallon caldron of hot water atop at all times. Our chef, M'ringi, a Kikuyu, had all the attributes of a culinary miracle worker, with recipes worthy of another gifted Kikuyun cook, Kamante, praised in Isak Dinesen's memoir.

Sunday, August 21, 1994

The Maasai dropped by our field camp-place, interrupting a hot lamb curry lunch to sell their wares. I discuss symbolism and merchandise values with my savvy assistant Kahare Miano, a native Kenyan of the Kikuyu tribe.

Tapping into the world of pleasure, people at play, call it man at his leisure—this fascination with prime-time big-time sports, the escalating wave of gambling casino addiction, fashionable restaurants, and bar-going, plus resort action—it all adds up to purchased entertainment serving a seemingly insatiable desire that human beings have to be diverted.

Purchased entertainment, pay-to-play, leisure and pleasure activities are all outlets for man's constant need for social distractions. The trick is to pick wisely from among many as the most suitable distractions at a price. It's a matter of voluntary selection—cost often doesn't seem to enter into it.

The safari provides exactly that sort of experience—a luxurious and expensive adventure at an exclusive private game preserve is a value worth every dollar invested.

More than exciting, the safarist finds the experience truly rewarding. Like art, everything you put into it gives full return. The wild animals, in a life of freedom and independence, are available as subjects in a setting where only reality prevails.

Heading out from Nairobi in 1909, Teddy Roosevelt set off the Big Game hunting craze. Today in Kenya all shooting has ceased. No more gun carriers—only camera carriers. Today a good photograph shot in the bush is as admired as yesterday's mounted heads and animal skins.

So too with a painting. The opportunity to be mobile and drive over uncharted terrain is a quest to discover for yourself and sketch these magnificent beasts, and then to erect an easel constructed specially for the project and commence painting right out there in the open, in their backyard.

Now we can get down to discussing the work and its process.

Once my working location had been determined, the clean white canvas that had been stretched in New York, then shipped, was erected with the help of our drivers, guide, cook's helpers, and Kahare. Reacting to the dramatic surroundings, I covered the surface excitedly with raw color.

I had already been sketching in the bush for several days and was impatient to get going, immersed as I now was in the strange unfamiliar environs. The color impact and the intense quality of the light grabs you. Having no particular design or composition in mind, I worked myself spontaneously into an abstract maze of paint from which the Big Five would eventually evolve.

An impression of a giant bull elephant emerged first out of the confusion of pigment. I just couldn't get myself to push him back into the middle distance to increase the scale of the other animals—being so large he remained a sort of centerpiece. A congested area of paint in the upper left corner suggested where the leopard in a tree belonged. The right foreground was an ideal prime position for the enthroned lions to pose. The rhinoceros and cape buffalo just dropped in naturally.

We hauled the canvas around, moving from site to site as I added impressions, deleted areas, and moved Mt. Kenya about—adding zebra, then cheetah, and even managing to include giraffe in the far distance.

To set the stage for the painting drama, allow me to present the cast of characters starring the Big Five—the Lion, the Elephant, the Cape Buffalo, the Rhinoceros, and the Leopard, plus cameos by the Cheetah, the Zebra, and the Giraffe.

A huge stomping bull elephant dominates the center area of the diptych. With earth-shaking footfalls he cuts a swath through the tall grass, ears flapping full sail.

The post-dining naps of two passive, well-fed purring lions are disrupted as a long line of pachyderms follows the leader, plodding and swaying steadily, as they trail along behind.

To the left of the centerpiece elephant, an awe-inspiring, massive, prehistoric rhinoceros couple graze unconcerned, grunting and snorting. They are probably lovers in hopes of procreating to increase this crucially endangered species.

You can be sure the cagey, meat-eating leopard camouflaged overhead, will not mess with them. Rhino are best left alone, they can be violent and destructive when frightened or angered. The idea is just to stay clear. Anyway, rhino have no place on the leopard's menu.

So the solitary leopard clad in its luxurious spotted coat, a smart and graceful scoundrel, just won't jump rhino with their two-inch thick skin. The texture of rhino hide is so rugged, weathered, and cruddy you'd think the very ones you're looking at right now are thousands of years old.

MAASAI

LeRoy Neiman

a banquet possibility if spotted by a pride of lions.

In the narrative right half of the painting such a situation has occurred. A pride of lions scattered about in tall grass stealthily surrounds an aging bull who has wandered away and is cut off from the herd.

The hungry lions slink along on their bellies stalking their prey, bent on doing him in. It's a veritable mine field.

This second half of the diptych I painted in my studio upon my return. I hadn't intended an extension but became hooked on a lingering memory experienced one afternoon when we happened upon this scene. I decided on a narrative painting of the unfolding of a potential tragedy, calling on sketches of the lions made during that three-hour vigil we spent sweating out the outcome. These studies are reproduced on pages 30–31, 34–35, and 36–37.

The old buff, alert and aware of deadly danger, freezes. His only choices are to charge or take off. In a community effort several lions could jump him, dig in their claws, and bring him down.

Such is the drama of the bush.

I will leave it up to you, dear viewer-reader, to determine the buffalo's eventful fate. Will he fall victim to sanguinary consequences? Or will he miraculously escape?

LAND

Maasai

In *The Green Hills of Africa,* 1935, Ernest Hemingway wrote about the Maasai, "They were the tallest, best built, handsomest people I had ever seen and the first truly happy people I had seen in Africa."

LeRoy Neiman
Maasai Mara

The tranquillity of the shepherd
Cattle provide nourishment —
Meat, blood and milk - and skins
Ritual sacrifice

The Maasai are a semi-nomadic pastoral people that roam primarily in Kenya and Tanzania. They live in harmony with plains animals in a setting of often parched, open spaces. They are custodians of domestic livestock, shepherding vast herds of cattle, sheep, or goats—the only meat they eat.

Only predators that endanger their herds are hunted and killed. Lion hunting is a symbol of courage.

A Maasai male's most-valued possession is his spear. It is always in hand. He leans on it while guarding the cattle or whenever striking a pose.

The Maasai, elegant in bearing and manner, will neither lie nor thieve. Tall, slim, long-headed, they bear themselves proudly. Handsome, aware of their good looks, they enhance themselves by adorning their bodies intricately. They are brave, brilliant, fearless, athletic, arrogant, confident, courageous, adventurous flirts, and rumored to be great lovers. Lion hunters—the lion may run faster, but the Maasai can run longer. They truly love to run.

Below: Warriors pose with all the confidence and style of their physical presence.

The Maasai are much the same as a thousand years ago. Resisting change they live the same ancient style.

Of the 50 languages spoken in Kenya the unifying tongues are Kiswahili and English. The Maasai speak their native Ol-Maa.

The beauty of the Africans comes from their keenness. Africans, man and animal, are particularly alert—the result of many generations of hunting and being hunted. Their stances and postures are always aware and ready, ever-scenting, ever-listening—a snake slithering silently, the leopard out on a limb, the touchy rhino, the easily irritated elephant, the stealthy, padding big cats, the neighboring warrior. The heads of man and beast cock at the faintest sound, the eyes glisten and sparkle. They are attuned. It is a beautiful attitude.

The warrior (*moran*) in full dress war gear may be attired in a headdress of gleaming black ostrich feathers or lions' manes, elaborate patterned shields of buffalo hides, spears glistening and gleaming in the sun. They style their hair, paint their legs, ornament themselves with beads, paint white chalk and varied red chalk colors on their bodies, all this for ceremonial occasions.

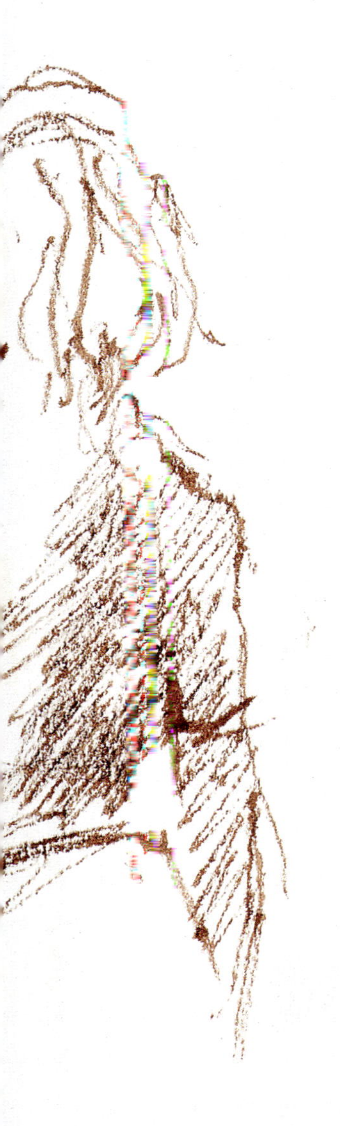

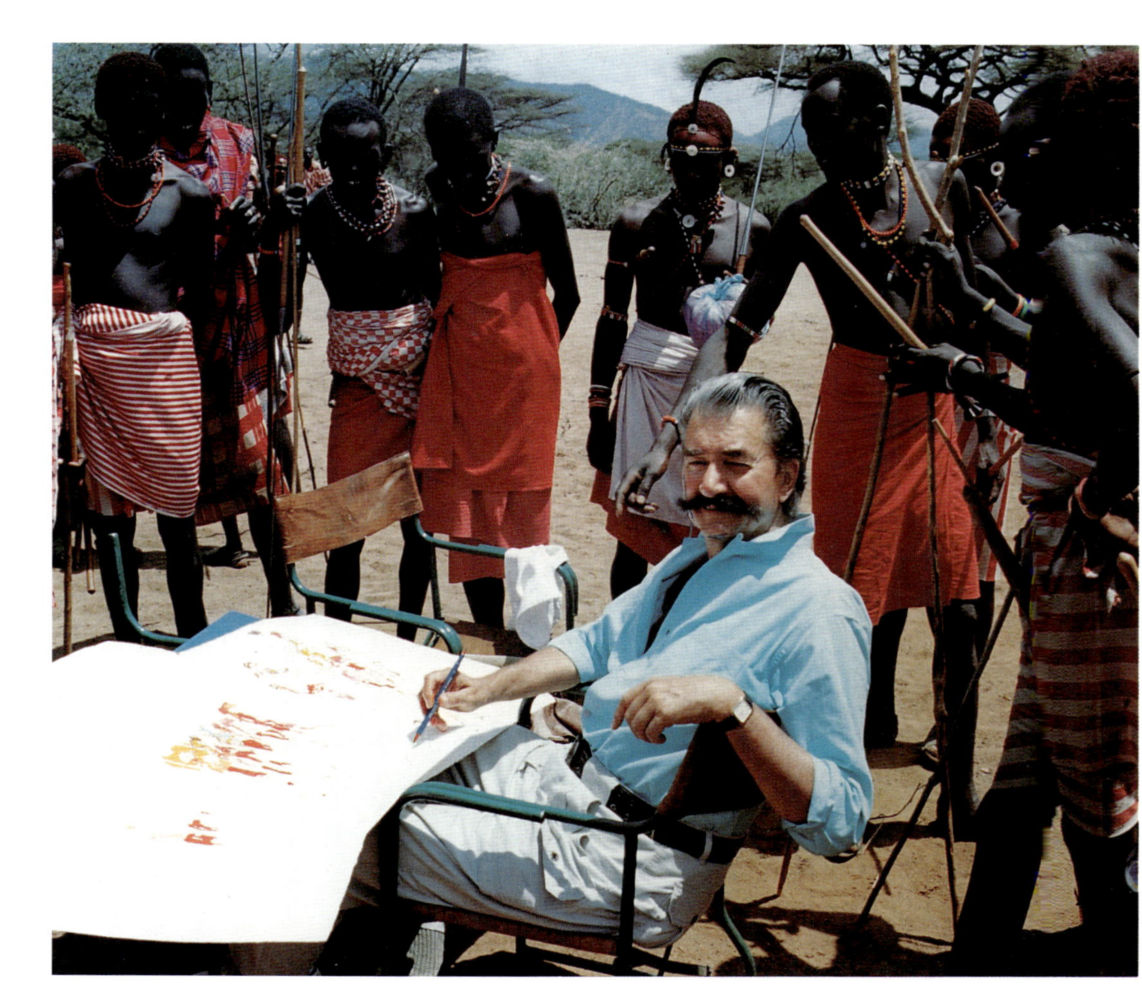

Native ritual dances bring out raw emotions that frequently escalate to a frenzy. This is emphasized by a rhythmic breathy chant composed of harsh, guttural sounds. In Maasai jumping dances, shoulders tremble at the height of the effortless jump with dazzling hang time. In these dances, the warlike spirit of the Maasai is revealed in all its evocative force.

Maasai Mara
LeRoy Neiman '94

'94
Kenya

The Maasai display plenty of vanity to be sure. But the pure naturalness of their lean, graceful, splendidly proportioned bodies says no Nautilus machines or steroids here.

A final word about the Maasai. Warriors pierce their ears and smear their bodies with varied decorative patterns. They establish individuality with imagination to appear terrifying to an enemy or to arouse their women's admiration. The young beauties respond by singing of getting married and raising healthy, handsome children. They work on beads for necklaces and earrings to adorn themselves, to appear provocative and desirable.

(Right and below)
Two 1970 safari sketches of Maasai maidens.

Epilogue

Human fascination with animals goes back to the dawn of time. Prehistoric man left impressive paintings of a wide variety of animals on the walls of caves. Many of these paintings appeared in Africa during the Stone Age, inspired by daily life. Though the practice of the arts began with prehistoric man, art as a profession is of more recent origin.

In other centuries, the beasts of Africa were magnificently interpreted by the great artists working from imagination, hearsay, and from animals in captivity. It is unlikely that the "old masters" ever saw the wild animals that they painted in such a lifelike manner in their natural environment, doubtful that Peter Paul Rubens, who stressed such violence in his lion hunt oils, ever actually saw such action live. One wonders what they would have come up with had they had such an opportunity.

Today's artists have these great works at their disposal to study, but more exciting is the access to the real and glorious four-footed creatures who are available to be portrayed with little or no accompanying danger in the wilds of Africa.

Ours was a twenty-day venture. Exhausted but fulfilled, our mission accomplished, we folded up our tents and returned to Nairobi, checked into the Norfolk Hotel, paused in the bar, dined at The Carnivore on herbivore, piscivore, and a bit of boozivore . . . and after visiting the Natural History Museum—which included beholding the exalted Elephant Ahmed renowned for having had the largest ivories ever known—took off the next day for New York City.

I took leave of Africa with a special salute to its magnetic animals and people. With a special thanks to the fascinating and incomparable lion, elephant, cape buffalo, rhinoceros, and leopard. The Big Five.

Safari Friends

Aboard the Hummer in the wilds with film producer Robert Halmi, Sr., and amanuensis Lynn Quayle.

With a baboon acquaintance in the Maasai Mara.

With my amiable aide-de-camp, Kahare.

A surprise encounter in Nairobi with photographer Annie Leibowitz . . . she on her way to Rwanda, I having just returned from the bush.

List of Plates

All dimensions are shown here in inches.

Acknowledgments and Photo Credits

Many thanks to Patty Otis Abel for her editorial assistance, and to Lynn Quayle for her participation in preparing the text.

All photographs of art by Anthony Holmes and Camerarts, Inc.
All other photographs by Lynn Quayle except:
Photographs on pages 27 and 151 by Robert Halmi, Sr.
Photograph on page 161, top, by Mary Elkins.